FUN SCIENCE EXPERIMENTS

FUN SCIENCE EXPERIMENTS WITH PLANTS

Claudia Martin

Illustrated by Annie Wilkinson

WINDMILL BOOKS

Published in 2025 by Windmill Books,
an Imprint of Rosen Publishing
2544 Clinton St.
Buffalo, NY 14224

First published in Great Britain in 2022 by Wayland

Author: Claudia Martin
Illustrator: Annie Wilkinson
Designer: Clare Nicholas
Series Designer: Rocket Design (East Anglia) Ltd

Cataloging-in-Publication Data

Names: Martin, Claudia, author. | Wilkinson, Annie, illustrator.
Title: Fun science experiments with plants / by Claudia Martin, illustrated by Annie Wilkinson.
Description: Buffalo, New York : Windmill Books, 2025. | Series: Fun science experiments | Includes glossary and index.
Identifiers: ISBN 9781538396551 (pbk.) | ISBN 9781538396568 (library bound) | ISBN 9781538396575 (ebook)
Subjects: LCSH: Plants--Experiments--Juvenile literature. | Botany--Experiments--Juvenile literature. | Science projects--Juvenile literature.
Classification: LCC QK49.M37 2025 | DDC 580.78--dc23

Printed in the United States of America

CPSIA Compliance Information: Batch #CSWM25. For Further Information contact Rosen Publishing at 1-800-237-9932

SAFETY PRECAUTIONS

We recommend adult supervision at all times while doing the experiments in this book. Always be aware that ingredients may contain allergens, so check the packaging for allergens if there is a risk of an allergic reaction. Anyone with a known allergy must avoid these.

* Wash your hands with soap and water after touching plants or seeds.
* Wear gloves when gardening.
* Do not put seeds or other plant parts in your mouth.
* Ask an adult for help with cutting.
* Cover surfaces with plastic or newspaper.

CONTENTS

Give plant science a try!

Caring for plants is an amazing way to learn about science. When you are gardening, you are carrying out experiments more often than you think!

Watering a plant or moving its pot from shade to sunlight are experiments that tell us all about what plants need to survive. When you carefully tuck soil around a plant's roots, you are setting up an experiment into how plants draw up the materials they need from the soil. When you eat a homegrown bean or carrot, you are showing how important plants are to people.

Gardening is a perfect way to learn about biology, the branch of science that studies living things and their life cycles. For example, we can learn about the life cycle of flowering plants. They begin life as seeds, sprout into plants, and produce flowers. The flowers may be visited by a bee carrying pollen, then produce seeds. Healthy plants are essential for a healthy planet, so plant science is more important than ever before.

BECOME A SCIENTIST

Science is not about knowing all the answers; it is about asking questions, coming up with a possible answer (called a hypothesis), then testing the hypothesis through experiments. Even famous scientists get things wrong, so they talk to other scientists then try again. A hypothesis is like a seed, which may grow into a tall tree – or may not. When a plant does not grow well, gardeners talk to each other, then plant more seeds.

When trying the experiments in this book, work as a team. Try to predict the results, and ask yourself what would happen if you did something differently. Record your results by taking photos or making drawings. A healthy, green plant to show off to friends and family is the best result of all!

DO YOUR OWN THING

You can add your own twist to all the experiments in this book. Try decorating your own plant pots, which you could make from the containers in your recycling. You could grow vegetables or give your plants as gifts.

Amazing maze

In this experiment, we will design a mystifying maze. While we watch a young bean plant travel through the maze, we will find out about what plants need to survive.

You will need

- An adult to help you
- Cardboard box with a lid attached
- Plant pot (no bigger than a quarter of the size of your box)
- Runner bean seed (never put seeds in your mouth)
- Soil
- Water
- Thick black cardboard
- Ruler
- Scissors
- Sticky tape

1. Fill your plant pot with soil, leaving a couple of inches at the top. Plant your bean seed 1–1 ½ inches (3–4 cm) beneath the soil surface. Add a little water. If you are working as a team, everyone can plant their own seed. If some do not sprout, share the ones that do!

2. Leave your plant pot on a warm windowsill for around one week, until the seed starts to sprout. Add a little water when the soil feels dry.

3. Turn your box on its side, so the lid is facing the front. One side of the box is now the "top" of your maze. Toward the left side of the "top," draw a square around 2 inches (5 cm) wide. **Ask an adult** to cut out this square. This is tricky, so do not try it yourself.

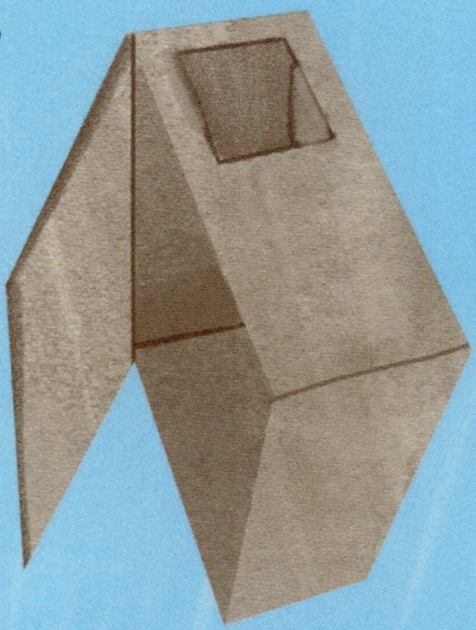

4. Measure the length and width of the "top" of your maze. On your black cardboard, draw a rectangle that is 3/4 inch (2 cm) longer and 3/4 inch (2 cm) wider than the "top." Cut out your rectangle.

5. Now fold a 3/4-inch-wide (2-cm) flap along one long side of your rectangle. Then fold a ½-inch (1-cm) flap along both short sides.

6 **!** Draw a square 2 inches (5 cm) wide on the right side of your black rectangle. **Ask an adult** to help you cut it out.

DO YOUR OWN THING

Try creating a plant sculpture by placing several bean plants in a cardboard box. Ask an adult to cut lots of holes in the sides and top of the box. Paint the outside of your box in bold colors. Watch as the plants create a living work of art!

7 Put your plant pot in the bottom of your maze, on the left. Position your black rectangle in the box, at least 2 inches (5 cm) above the top of your plant pot. Fix the card in place by taping the flaps to the sides of the box.

8 Close the lid of the box. Carefully place your maze in a warm, sunny spot.

9 Over the next two weeks, open the door of your maze every day to see how your plant is growing. What do you notice? Why do you think your plant is growing in this way? Water your plant regularly.

What happened and why?

Our runner bean plant grew toward the sunlight. Plants need sunlight to survive because they turn the sun's energy into food energy.

Plants make their own food using a process called photosynthesis (which means "making from light" in ancient Greek). Sunlight is energy given off by the sun. Plants soak up sunlight using a green chemical called chlorophyll. This is why their leaves are green!

Plants also take in water (which you gave your plant) and carbon dioxide, which is a gas they absorb from the air. Using the energy from sunlight, plants change carbon dioxide and water into sugar and another gas, oxygen.

WHAT DO YOU THINK?

If you did not water your plant, what would happen? If you covered the top hole of your maze, would your plant survive?

How did our plant grow toward the sunlight, since it has no eyes to see the light? Plants make a chemical called auxin, which reacts to sunlight. On the sunnier side of our plant's stem, the auxin was broken down by the sunlight. On the shady side, the auxin encouraged the plant's cells to grow bigger. This made the plant bend toward the light.

AUXIN IN ACTION

Auxin encourages plants to grow. As well as making plants grow toward sunlight, auxin helps their roots grow downward. Auxin responds to the pull of gravity, the force that pulls all objects to the center of Earth. Auxin collects in the lowest tips of roots, making them grow farther downward.

Bubble bubble

Did you know that plants blow bubbles? We are going to count the bubbles made by pondweed, which is a water plant. Those bubbles will tell us more about photosynthesis.

You will need

- An adult to help you
- *Elodia* pondweed (buy in an aquarium shop or online)
- Lamp with a bright LED bulb
- A glass
- Water at room temperature
- 20-inch (50-cm) ruler or tape measure
- Scissors
- Stopwatch
- Pencil
- Paper

1 ! **Ask an adult** to help with this experiment, as electricity and water are a dangerous combination. Never touch the light with wet hands. Keep water away from sockets.

2 If you cannot use your pondweed right after buying, keep it in a shallow container of water, in full sunlight. Use as soon as possible.

3 Cut a piece of pondweed around 2 ½ inches (7 cm) long. Make sure it has healthy leaves and only one cut end. Place your pondweed in a glass with the cut end facing upward. Pour water into the glass until all the pondweed is underwater.

4 Place your ruler on a table. Position the glass of pondweed next to 0 inches on the ruler. Position your lamp with its bulb close to the glass.

5 Turn on the lamp. Close the curtains or blinds.

6 After 1 or 2 minutes, you should see bubbles rising from the cut end of the pondweed stem. If bubbles stop appearing, cut the end of the stem again.

7 Start the stopwatch. Count how many bubbles you see rising from the stem in 1 minute. Write down your results.

8 ❗ **Ask an adult** to move the lamp to 4 inches (10 cm) from the glass of pondweed. Wait 5 minutes for the pondweed to get used to the change in light. Then start the stopwatch and count the bubbles you see in one minute.

9 Repeat Step 8 with the lamp at 8, 12, 16, and 20 inches (20, 30, 40, and 50 cm) from the pondweed.

10 Can you see a pattern in your results? What do you think caused the change?

DO YOUR OWN THING

When you have finished your experiment, do not plant your pondweed outdoors, as it is invasive. This means it can spread out of control. Instead, you could grow it in a glass bowl indoors. Plant it in 2 inches (5 cm) of colored stones at the bottom of the bowl, then fill with water to create a water garden.

What happened and why?

The closer the lamp was to the pondweed, the more the pondweed bubbled. The bubbles were oxygen, a gas that plants make during photosynthesis.

When plants photosynthesize (see page 8), they turn sunlight, carbon dioxide, and water into sugar and oxygen. They use some of the oxygen to break down the sugar for energy. They release any oxygen they do not need.

When there is more sunlight, plants photosynthesize faster. At night, they stop. We can tell the pondweed was photosynthesizing faster in bright light because it was making more oxygen!

WHAT DO YOU THINK?

Based on your results, what do you think would happen if you moved the lamp to 3 feet (1 m) from the pondweed? Would the pondweed bubble?

OXYGEN IN ACTION

Humans and other animals need to breathe in oxygen from the air because, like plants, we use it to release energy from food. Before tiny living things began photosynthesizing around 2.5 billion years ago, there was little or no oxygen in Earth's atmosphere. Without plants, we would not be able to breathe!

Land plants absorb carbon dioxide from the air, but water plants absorb it from water. Although we cannot see them do it, land plants release their waste oxygen from tiny holes in their leaves. Water plants store some oxygen in their stems, so they float close to the water's surface, where there is more sunlight. Since we cut the stem of our pondweed, we could watch as it made oxygen.

Sucking up

We know that plants die without water. We are going to find out how plants suck up the water they need from the soil – while we make a crazily colorful stick of celery!

You will need

- An adult to help you
- Stick of celery with leaves
- Glass or jar
- Water
- Dark blue gel food coloring
- Table knife

1 ❗ **Ask an adult to help** you cut 1 inch (2 cm) off the bottom of your celery stick.

2 Pour water into your glass until it is about one-third full.

3 Add around one teaspoon of food coloring to your water, until it is dark and strongly colored. Add more coloring if needed. We are using dark blue because it will make the most dramatic effect.

4 Put the cut end of the celery stick into the glass. Make sure the stick is not so tall that it will tip over the glass.

5 You may start to see changes in your celery after half an hour, but for best results leave it in the glass for at least one hour. What changes can you see? What do you think has happened?

6 When you can see definite changes in your celery leaves, remove the stick from the water.

! **Ask an adult to help** you cut the celery stem in half. Examine the inside. What do you see? Discuss your observations with your team.

DO YOUR OWN THING

If you can buy six white carnations or other white flowers, try dyeing them different colors of the rainbow. Fill six jars with water, then add 20 drops of a different food coloring to each glass: red, orange, yellow, green, blue, and purple. Place the stem of one flower in each glass, then leave overnight.

What happened and why?

The process of water traveling through a plant is called transpiration. By adding food coloring to water, we were able to watch it happen.

Plants need water for photosynthesis (see page 8). Water also carries food around the plant: sugar made in the leaves and nutrients found in the soil. The water travels upward from the rain-soaked soil, through small tubes in a plant's roots, stem, and leaves.

Even though our celery stem was no longer attached to its roots, it still sucked up water from the glass. The food color dyed its leaves and its tubes, which are called xylem (pronounced zy-lum).

Water always flows downward, so how do plants make water travel upward from the soil? The answer is transpiration. This process is possible because plants lose water through tiny holes in their leaves, called stomata. The water evaporates (turns to gas) and floats into the air. As a molecule (tiny portion) of water evaporates from a leaf, it pulls on the next water molecule, creating a flow of water through the plant.

WHAT DO YOU THINK?

Now that you know plants lose water from their leaves, what do you think would happen if you tied a clear plastic bag around a leafy tree branch for a day?

TRANSPIRATION IN ACTION

Cacti usually live in deserts, where it rarely rains. In dry places, plants need to transpire less, so they do not run out of water. Many cacti do not have true leaves; they have spines, which do not have stomata. A thick covering of spines protects the stem from animals and from sunlight. Cacti carry out photosynthesis in their thick stems, which have very small stomata. The stomata stay closed during the hot day, opening only at night.

Magic beans

Most plants start life as a seed. A seed will start to sprout, or germinate, only when conditions are right. Let's find out about those conditions by trying to grow ... beanstalks!

You will need

- An adult to help you
- 12 runner bean seeds (never put seeds in your mouth)
- 4 resealable freezer bags
- 3 pieces of paper towel
- Water
- Sticky tape
- Refrigerator

1. Place three dry bean seeds in a freezer bag. Make sure there is a bit of air in the bag, then close it. Using sticky tape, attach the bag to a sunny window.

2. Wet a piece of paper towel, then place it in a freezer bag. Place three bean seeds onto the wet paper towel. As before, make sure there is some air in the bag, then close it. Stick this bag to a sunny window, next to your first bag if possible.

3. Wet a piece of paper towel, then place it in your third freezer bag. Place three bean seeds in this bag, close it (leaving some air inside), then put the bag in a dark cabinet.

4. Wet a piece of paper towel, then place it in your fourth freezer bag. Place your last three bean seeds in the bag. Close the bag, keeping some air inside, then place this bag in a refrigerator.

5 Discuss the conditions in each bag with your team. Do you think the conditions in all the bags are right for the seeds to grow?

6 Check on your seeds every day to see if they have grown. It may take around a week before you see any signs of germination. Since seeds are not perfectly reliable, we put three seeds in each bag to make sure at least one will grow, if the conditions in its bag are suitable.

7 After some of your seeds have germinated, can you see any differences between the growing seedlings in different bags?

DO YOUR OWN THING

When your seeds have sprouted, make pots for growing your bean plants using old juice or milk cartons. Ask an adult to cut off the tops of the cartons. Paint the outside of the cartons or wrap them in colored paper.

What happened and why?

Our seeds needed both warmth and water to crack their coating, allowing them to grow. As shown by the seeds in the cabinet, seeds do not need sunlight to germinate.

The seeds in the refrigerator did not germinate. Seeds will not germinate if it is too cold for young plants to survive. Only the warm seeds on wet paper towel were able to germinate. All our seeds also had some oxygen in their bags, which they need to release energy (see page 12) from the food stores contained in the seed.

The seeds in the cabinet germinated as fast as the seeds in the window. Most seeds start to grow in the dark under the soil, where they can spread their roots. However, as the cupboard seedlings grew, they were white, not green. Sunlight is needed for chlorophyll to develop.

Seeds are made by a flowering plant after a flower has been pollinated. Pollination is when pollen is carried from the male parts (stamens) of a flower to the female part (pistil) of a flower. The pollen may be carried by wind, water, or bees and other animals. Seeds grow in a fruit, which can be edible (such as an apple or peanut) or not edible (such as a dry, floating dandelion fruit). Pollination is a type of sexual reproduction because it needs both a male and a female plant.

WHAT DO YOU THINK?

What would happen to your cabinet-germinated seedlings if you left them in the cabinet for several weeks?

GERMINATION IN ACTION

Eucalyptus trees have seeds with such tough coatings that they germinate only after being melted by fire. These trees grow in Australia, where wildfires are common. Wildfires destroy plants that stop eucalyptus seedlings from getting sunlight. Adult eucalyptus trees recover quickly from fires.

Cabbage clone

Let's grow a cabbage clone, which is a new plant that is a copy of its lone parent. This is a type of asexual (or nonsexual) reproduction because it does not need both male and female plants.

You will need

An adult to help you
1 Savoy cabbage or similar
4 resealable freezer bags
4 pieces of paper towel
Sharp knife
Water
Pen

1. Pull all the leaves off your cabbage. We need only one leaf for this experiment, so for an idea of how to use all the others, see the "Do Your Own Thing" box.

2. Dampen four pieces of paper towel. Do not make them dripping wet.

3. Label your four freezer bags: "Leaf," "Top stem," "Middle stem," and "Bottom stem."

4. Wrap a cabbage leaf in one of the wet kitchen towels, then put it in the "Leaf" bag. Leaving some air inside, close the bag.

5. ❗ **Ask an adult** to cut the cabbage stem into three pieces crossways: bottom, middle, and top. Do not get the pieces mixed up.

6 Wrap each slice of cabbage stem in a wet paper towel, then place them in the "Top stem," "Middle stem," and "Bottom stem" bags. Leaving some air inside, close the bags.

7 Put all four bags in a sunny spot, at room temperature. Do you think all your cabbage pieces will start to grow into baby cabbages?

8 Every day for a week, open your bags to see if there are any changes. Can you see new leaves or roots? Wet your paper towels a little if they have dried out.

9 After a week, discuss your cloning results with your team!

DO YOUR OWN THING

Use your cabbage leaves to make coleslaw. Ask an adult to thinly slice the leaves, then mix in 8 tablespoons of mayonnaise, 2 tablespoons of cider vinegar, 2 tablespoons of mustard, and a sprinkle of salt and pepper. Do not eat if you are allergic to any of the ingredients.

What happened and why?

Your cabbage leaf began to rot, but the stem slices started to grow tiny new leaves and roots. The top of the cabbage stem probably grew best of all!

Many plants can reproduce either sexually or asexually. Depending on the conditions, they will use either method. We learned about sexual reproduction in flowering plants on page 21. A baby plant made by sexual reproduction has characteristics from both the male parent and the female parent. In contrast, asexual reproduction is when a plant makes a copy of itself, without help from another plant.

Not every part of a plant can reproduce asexually. In our cabbage, the tissue at the tip of the stem, where it grows a new stem, leaves, and buds, was able to start growing into a new plant best of all.

WHAT DO YOU THINK?

What would happen if you planted the top piece of cabbage stem in a pot with some soil?

There are two main ways that plants reproduce asexually. Some, such as strawberries and spider plants, grow long horizontal stems called runners. Baby plants grow at the ends of the runners. Some plants, such as onions and potatoes, store food in swollen underground leaves or stems called bulbs or tubers. These can grow into new plants.

ASEXUAL REPRODUCTION IN ACTION

Farmers often use asexual reproduction to grow new plants. If a tomato plant grows particularly tasty tomatoes, a farmer can take a "cutting" of a side shoot, then plant it. The new plant will make delicious tomatoes just like its parent.

Jungle jar

In our last experiment, we will find out about the water cycle. We will create a gorgeous garden in a jar that – after the first day – will never need watering.

You will need

An adult to help you
Large jar or bowl
Small cup or container
Handful of gravel
Soil or compost
Little plants
Old spoon or small trowel
Water
Cling wrap

1. For this experiment, you will need a transparent (see-through) plastic or glass jar or bowl that is big enough for you to reach inside to plant your "jungle." Your small cup or container should fit inside the jar, leaving room around it for your plants. Hopefully you can find suitable items among your recycling!

2. Put a 1-inch (2 ½-cm) layer of gravel at the bottom of your jar. This will help excess water drain away from your plants' roots.

3. Cover the gravel with 2–4 inches (5–10 cm) of soil.

4. Using an old spoon or small trowel, dig holes for your plants in the soil. Remember to leave room for your small container in the middle of the jar. Make your holes slightly bigger than the root balls of your plants. Rest your plants in their holes, then gently fill in around them with sprinklings of soil.

5 Water your plants so the soil feels damp to touch but is not soggy.

6 Fill your small container with water, then place it in the center of your "jungle."

7 Cover the top of your jar with cling wrap.

8 Put your jar in a warm, sunny spot. Leave for days or weeks, but take a look at your jungle jar regularly. What is happening to the water in the container? Are your plants green and healthy?

DO YOUR OWN THING

Turn your jungle jar into a dinosaur or fairy garden. Decorate any bare soil with colored stones, then add plastic dinosaurs or fairies. Create your own *Tyrannosaurus* or enchanted mushroom using cardboard and felt-tips. It will be damp inside your jar, so you will need to change paper decorations regularly.

What happened and why?

In your jungle jar, you created a mini planet Earth with its own "ocean" of water. Like on Earth, the water kept moving in an endless cycle, watering your plants along the way.

On Earth, water is constantly moving between the air, soil, and oceans. When the sun warms oceans, rivers, and lakes, some water evaporates, which means it turns into an invisible gas called water vapor. The water vapor rises in the warm air.

As the air rises, it cools. Cold air cannot hold as much water vapor as warm air, so some water vapor condenses. This means it turns into drops of liquid water, forming a cloud. When the water drops get too heavy to float, they fall as rain. This is called precipitation.

The water cycle constantly recycles water.

WHAT DO YOU THINK?

What would happen if you kept your jungle jar cold by putting it in a bucket of ice?

As you watched your jar, you saw that the water slowly disappeared from the small container as it evaporated. You probably saw water condensing on the cling wrap across the top of the jar, then falling like rain onto the soil.

The plants used this water for photosynthesis (see page 8), so they stayed green and healthy. The water cycle continued, as water evaporated from the wet soil and transpired (see pages 16–17) from the plants' leaves.

EARTH IN ACTION

A garden in a jar could survive for years without being opened, since the plants have water, sunlight, and carbon dioxide for photosynthesis. Will the air in the jar run out of carbon dioxide? Just like Earth, the jar should continue recycling its materials. Carbon dioxide will be released from the jar's soil as tiny living things within it feed on decaying material.

Glossary

absorb to take in or soak up

asexual reproduction when a plant or animal makes a copy of itself, without help from another plant or animal

atmosphere the blanket of gases that surrounds Earth

carbon dioxide a gas found in the atmosphere that is needed by plants to produce food

cell the smallest working part of a living thing

chlorophyll a green chemical found in plants that allows them to absorb sunlight

condense to change from a gas to a liquid

cutting a small part of a plant that is capable of growing into a new plant

edible eatable

evaporate to change from a liquid into a gas

fruit the part of a plant that contains seeds

germinate when a seed begins to grow and put out shoots

invasive able to spread quickly and harmfully

molecule a group of atoms that are bonded together; atoms are tiny portions of matter

nutrient a substance needed for growth

oxygen an invisible gas that is made by plants

photosynthesis the process by which plants produce food from sunlight, carbon dioxide, and water

pistil the female parts of a flower

pollen a powder made by the male parts of a flower

pollination the transfer of pollen from the male parts of a flower to the female parts, usually of another flower, which causes the female parts to make seeds

precipitation rain, snow, or hail

room temperature a comfortable indoor temperature

root the part of a plant that anchors it in position and takes in water and nutrients

stamen the male, pollen-making part of a flower

transpiration the process of water moving through a plant and being released from its leaves

water vapor water in the form of a gas

Further reading

BOOKS

Phenomenal Plants (Extreme Science),
Rob Colson and Jon Richards (Gareth Stevens, 2024)

Plants (Learn Science with Mo),
Paul Mason (Enslow Publishing, 2024)

Plants (Science Skills Sorted),
Angela Royston (Franklin Watts, 2019)

Q&A About Plants (Curious Nature),
Nancy Dickmann (PowerKids Press, 2018)

WEBSITES

Find out more about plants on these websites:

www.bbc.co.uk/bitesize/topics/zy66fg8

www.gardenersworld.com/how-to/grow-plants/10-gardening-projects-for-kids/

https:www.nhm.ac.uk/discover/plants.html

ww.kew.org/science/collections-and-resources/research-facilities/millennium-seed-bank

Index